CatL♥ve

CatL♥ve

210
Wonderful Things
You Can Do
For Your Cat

by

Jill Kramer

Hay House, Inc.
Carson, CA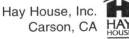

Published and distributed in the United States by:

Hay House, Inc., 1154 E. Dominguez St., P.O. Box 6204, Carson, CA 90749-6204   (800) 654-5126

The author of this book does not dispense medical advice or prescribe the use of any technique as a form of treatment for a cat's physical or medical problems without the advice of a veterinarian, either directly or indirectly. The intent of the author is only to offer information of a general nature. In the event you use any of the information in this book for yourself or your cat, which is your constitutional right, the author and the publisher assume no responsibility for your actions.

Book design: Christy Allison   Cover photo: Jill Kramer

Library of Congress Cataloging-in-Publication Data

Kramer, Jill (date)
         Catlove : 210 wonderful things you can do for your cat / by Jill Kramer.
            p.   cm.
   ISBN 1-56170-105-X (tradepaper) : $6.95
   1. Cats.   I. Title
   SF447.K73   1994
   636.8 ' 083—dc20   94-29059
                                                                           CIP

ISBN 1-56170-105-X

98 97 96 95 94   5 4 3 2 1
First Printing, November 1994

Printed in the United States of America

...And on the ninth day, God did sayeth:
"I shall summon My most beloved angels,
and shall incarnate them as feline creatures,
that they might provide loving companionship
for humankind on this Earth."

— Cat Proverb
Kramer 19:94

ON THE COVER – *Dolly "Cookie" Kramer,* age 2. Dolly was abandoned on a doorstep when she was a kitten, rescued by a kindly catlover, and then adopted by the author. (Isn't she a doll!)

To my mother, *Anne Kramer*, the ultimate cat mother of all cat mothers; and to my own little "angels," *Sage* and *Dolly*.

Dear Fellow CatL♥ver:

If you're like me, you view your cat as a cherished family member and not simply a "pet." My cats are my buddies, my pals, my little loves, my sweetie pies, and my beloved "children."

So, I have written a little book dedicated to the love of all cats—especially yours! I hope you will apply some of the "wonderful things" included within to your own cat's life and that you live a long and *purr*-fectly happy life with cats by your side.

So... ♫ To all the cats I've loved before...who've come purring at my door...I've loved you all so much...You're so much fun to touch...To all the cats I've loved before... ♫

(Okay, no more singing.)

Remember: The '90s are the ME-ow Generation, so L♥ve a Cat today!

Jill Kramer

P.S. I am aware that many of you have more than one cat, as I do, but I have used the singular word *cat* throughout most of the book for ease of usage. Also, I have referred to cats as both *"him"* and *"her,"* respectively, so that both *Toms* and *Thomasinas* will be represented equally.

ACKNOWLEDGMENTS

I gratefully acknowledge:

MY PUBLISHER, EMPLOYER, AND FRIEND, *Louise L. Hay*, for the wonderful opportunities that she has given me, and for all the *positive*-ly amazing things that she *has* done and *is* doing in her life—not only for the two- and four-legged creatures who walk *above* the Earth, but also for the trees, plants, and flowers that grow *from* it. I send great big hugs to Louise's beautiful Himalayan cat, *Sabrina*; to her beloved canine cuties, *Frances, Winkie*, and *Hyland*; and to her sweet little bunny wabbits, *Mitsie* and *Bitsie*.

MY DEAR FRIEND THROUGHOUT MANY LIVES (remember ancient Egypt?), *Christy Allison*, for her love, inspiration, and creative input on this book; and a special kiss to her "goodgirls," *Tabitha Hay Allison* and *Lily* (the little stinker).

MY TALENTED FRIEND, *Mark Kingsley Brown*, whose wonderful illustrations purr-fectly captured the love I have for my own cats...and ALL felines.

MY OTHER FRIENDS AND RELATIVES WHO ARE CRAZY ABOUT THEIR *CATS* (and ALL animals):

Anne Kramer and *Snowshoes*; Jacquie, Bob, and Max Harris and *Gretel Granola* and *Lucy Boots* (and long-lost *Sneakers*); Amy Huggins and *Hank Jr.* and *Buddy*; Jeff, Elsa, and Hayley Rosenberg and *Whitney, Woody, Soupy*, and *Maah-Maah* (and the late great *Pissmeyer, Wanda*, and *Kissie*); Stormy Weber Vogel and *Mazie*; Randi and Dave Selleck and *Bubba* and *Tigger*; Mary Ann Bastian and the next cat in her life; Reid Tracy and *Chelsea*; Jeannie Liberati and *Tuffy, Sandy*, and *Gata*; Krysta Stark and *Sasha*; Polly Tracy and *Punkie, Brewster*, and *Skinny*; Doreen Virtue and *Romeo*; Robert Odom and *Buffy, Sissy*, and *Jodie Marie*; and to all the other cat♥vers at Hay House: Carol, Gary, Robert, Joe, Eddie, Cynthia, Kimberly, Kristina, and Ron and his pooch (and our Hay House mascot) *Heidi*!

I love all of you...and your *pets*!

❈ CatL♥ve 1 ❈

How about getting your little angel a kitty companion. She'll love the company when you're at work or out of town, and the difference between feeding one cat and two will barely make a dent in your budget...But don't despair if they fight like cats and dogs! for the first few weeks. This type of transition is to be expected.

❧ CatL♥ve 2 ❧

Brush or comb your cat every day. You will not only remove the excess fur that can give him all those nasty furballs, but grooming also stimulates circulation and oil-gland secretions in the skin, resulting in a shiny and beautiful coat. And while you're brushing or combing him, whisper sweet nothings in his cute little cat ears.

❧ CatL♥ve 3 ❧

*G*et on your cat's level and have some fun! You know exactly what she likes to play with—and it's probably a balled-up piece of newspaper as opposed to that $14.95 cat toy you bought last week. So, get down! She'll love you for it!

 CatL♥ve 4

You know that favorite sunny spot your cat likes to sleep on every afternoon? Make it a warm and comfortable napping place by laying down a soft blanket or pillow. <u>You</u> wouldn't want to sleep on a hard surface, would you?

❖ CatL♥ve 5 ❖

Whether your cat eats dry
food or wet or both, make sure
you give him some variety. No
self-respecting finicky cat wants
to eat beef and liver dinner
every day!

❖ CatL♥ve 6 ❖

If your cat scratches a lot, it's no fun for her, let me tell you (I know this because my cat told me so), so use a flea comb on a regular basis and vacuum and/or shampoo your rugs often. Some garlic in your cat's diet can help combat those pesky fleas, too.

❀ CatL♥ve 7 ❀

Form relationships with people who like cats. For example, before I will go out on a date with someone, I always ask the man how he feels about felines. If he sneers and says something like "I've never liked cats," that is the last I see of him! And if you happen to make a friend who does like cats but is allergic, suggest shots. Because people come and go, but cats (and all pets) are in there for the long haul!

❧ CatL♥ve 8 ❧

Let your cat sleep with you.
You'll enjoy the warmth and
companionship of a sweet, furry
body next to you in bed, and
sleeping together is a great way
for you and your cat to bond.
But don't move around too
much at night—you don't want
to wake kitty up, do you?

❖ CatL♥ve 9 ❖

If you live in a part of the country prone to natural disasters, make sure you have an evacuation plan that includes your cat. For example, when the 6.7 earthquake hit L.A. in '94, I quickly retrieved my cat carrier from an accessible part of my bedroom closet. Now, the fact that my cat didn't come out from under the dishwasher for two days did, I admit, present a separate dilemma, but at least I was prepared!

❧ CatL♥ve 10 ❧

The American dream is to own a home, correct? Well, your cat wants a home of his own, too. You can buy a nice three-level kitty condo at your local pet store. And just think—no 30-year mortgage to deal with!

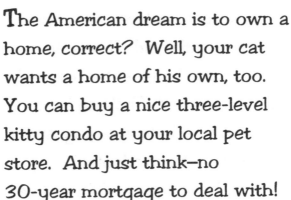

❧ CatL♥ve 11 ❧

Get your cat neutered as soon as he's six months old. If he's an outdoor cat, you'll prevent unwanted pregnancies, and if he's an indoor cat, you'll preclude spraying...and a lot of sexual frustration! (Female cats can be spayed at four or five months.)

❧ CatL♥ve 12 ❧

If your cat loves milk but you find that it sometimes upsets her system, try giving her skim (or 1%) milk a few times a month. It won't taste much different from whole milk to her, and she will probably be able to digest it better.

❧ CatL♥ve 13 ❧

Watch your feet when you walk around your home. Tripping over your cat hurts him as much as it does you!

❧ CatL♥ve 14 ❧

Give your cat a good lap to sit on. That's it—relax in a comfy chair, put a blanket over your knees, and let her have her way with you.

❀ CatL♥ve 15 ❀

I'm sure you've seen a little crusty material in your cat's eyes at times. Don't despair—just wipe his eyes (in the direction of the nose) with some wet cotton or tissue. Now he can clearly see...how much you love him!

❀ CatL♥ve 16 ❀

If you haven't gotten around to spaying your cat (and I'm sure you have a good excuse, right?), and your cat does have kittens, you've got six to eight weeks to find good homes for your cat's babies. Make it your number-one priority.

❧ CatL♥ve 17 ❧

You know how your cat seemingly disappears, and you search every nook and cranny in your home but you can't find her, and then after a few hours, there she is, and you can't figure out where her hiding place could have been? Well, the best thing you can do for your cat is to let her be. She does need her space, you know.

❧ CatL♥ve 18 ❧

If you have an indoor cat, make sure he gets some fresh air. If you don't have an enclosed patio or balcony, put a leash and harness on kitty, and take him outside for a few minutes every day. (Now, I must admit that my cat simply sank to the ground when I tried this, but maybe your cat will be more agreeable.)

❧ CatL♥ve 19 ❧

And now...a few words about litter boxes. Have you ever gone a whole day without flushing? Of course not! So, please don't make your cat suffer! Scoop out or change the litter at least once a day. It makes *scents*, doesn't it?

 CatL♥ve 20 ❧

You know how your cat always sits on the very section of the Sunday paper that you've just started to peruse? Well, let her. There are lots of other sections you can read instead.

❦ CatL♥ve 21 ❦

If your sweetie pie gets the runs, but has no other sign of illness, give him as much clean water as he wants, and avoid feeding him for a day or two. Then, when he's better, feed him very small portions of canned or dry cat food, or cooked meat (but no raw liver or milk, please!).

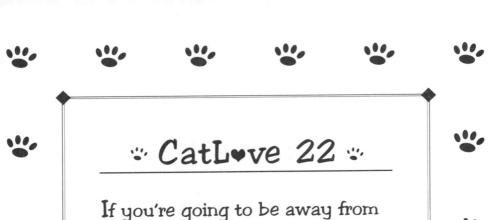

❧ CatL♥ve 22 ❧

If you're going to be away from home for much of the day, leave some tunes playing on the stereo so your cat can feel like he has some company...but no heavy metal...kitty can only take so much!

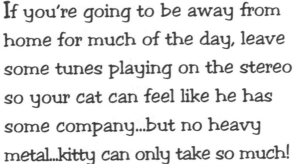

 CatL♥ve 23

If you want to keep track of your cat's appetite, feed her moderate amounts of food at about the same time each day. And if her canned food has been in the refrigerator, let it warm to room temperature before serving. There's nothing worse than cold, congealed kidney and liver dinner!

❀ CatL♥ve 24 ❀

When you go on a vacation, don't board your cat if you can help it. How would you like to sit in a cage for two weeks? For the same amount of money, you could probably pay a neighbor to take care of him.

❧ CatL♥ve 25 ❧

If you're reading this book but don't have a cat yet, please think about adopting one. I've often heard busy professionals say, "Well, it wouldn't be fair for me to get a cat; I only have a one-bedroom apartment, and I work all day." Well, my reply to that is: What's better—a cat living in a 3x5-foot cage in an animal shelter waiting to be put to sleep, or a cat who lives in a nice, warm apartment with plenty of food and water and...an owner who does come home at some point? Think about it.

 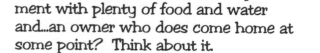

☀ CatL♥ve 26 ☀

If you're wondering what type of cat to adopt, quiet, long-haired cats tend to adapt better to apartment life, while shorter-haired cats are better in wide open spaces. But, this is not a hard-and-fast rule, so just love a cat—no matter how much hair she has!

❦ CatL♥ve 27 ❦

When you do adopt a cat, take him to a veterinarian immediately so he can be checked for feline leukemia, fleas, worms, and other maladies. If you have other pets at home, you wouldn't want your new baby to bring home any unwanted "gifts."

❧ CatL♥ve 28 ❧

When company comes over, put the tiniest dab of perfume on the very top of your cat's head (where she can't lick it off). Your guests will think you have the most *scent*-sational cat around, which may elicit some extra attention.

❧ CatL♥ve 29 ❧

Don't ever forget who's running the show. It's your cat's home. He just lets you live there. So be a good tenant, and pay all your bills on time. You wouldn't want the electricity to be turned off while you're at work. Kitty needs his heat and air conditioning!

☙ CatL♥ve 30 ☙

Talk to your cat often. It doesn't matter whether it's baby talk or grown-up talk or off-key singing or gibberish. She loves the sound of her Mommy or Daddy's voice!

❧ CatL♥ve 31 ❧

If your cat sleeps in a basket, box, or even a favorite chair most of the time, make sure you clean the blanket, pillow, or cushion regularly. You wouldn't want to sleep on the same sheets all the time, would you?

❖ CatL♥ve 32 ❖

If your cat has claws and spends most of its time indoors, get him a cat tree, a piece of cardboard, or a scratching post. If you don't, your upholstery will be his first choice!

❧ CatL♥ve 33 ❧

Learn your cat's unspoken language, so you can communicate with her better. For example, when she yawns, she's not necessarily sleepy; she's telling you she feels peaceful and content. And, when she slowly blinks her eyes at you, she's telling you she LOVES you!

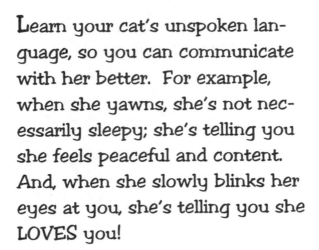

❧ CatL♥ve 34 ❧

If you have a long-haired cat, comb and brush him every day so his fur doesn't get matted—this is especially important in the spring and fall during shedding season.

❧ CatL♥ve 35 ❧

Avoid giving your cat any meat that may have bones in it, but you can give your cat treats from your table in moderation. Make sure you haven't overspiced the food, though. Kitty likes her food rather bland.

❧ CatL♥ve 36 ❧

Have you ever been tempted to give your cat some of your dog's food? Well, please don't! Dog food doesn't have the protein that cats need, so stick to the nutrient-rich cat food you get at your local pet store.

 CatL♥ve 37

Have you noticed that your cat loves nibbling on your plants? Well, you can keep him from doing this by planting some cat grass in a pot and letting him chew on that. Then you'll both be happy!

 CatL♥ve 38

Always have an abundant supply of litter on hand. Not only will your cat appreciate it, but it may come in handy for you if there's a natural disaster and the plumbing stops functioning. It also works great on icy driveways.

❄ CatL♥ve 39 ❄

When there are children in the vicinity of your cat, keep an eye on them. Pulling tails and otherwise terrorizing your puss may keep the kids in stitches...but kitty doesn't like it at all. Trust me on this!

❄ CatL♥ve 40 ❄

Give your cat a special treat today! How about some lean sliced turkey from the deli or some liver pâté? (But don't do it every day!)

 CatL♥ve 41

If you've been feeding your cat commercial cat food but would like to switch to the more nutritious stuff from the pet supply store, try mixing the new food in with the old gradually. If you start feeding him the new food exclusively, he will probably go on a hunger strike!

☙ CatL♥ve 42 ☙

Clean out your cat's food and water bowls every day. I've seen people refilling their cat's dry food bowls without washing them first, and I always think: Would _you_ use the same food dish every day without scrubbing it first? Of course not! Remember: cats are people, too!

❀ CatL♥ve 43 ❀

Catnip is fun, legal, and inexpensive, so give some to your cat from time to time. I mean, it's not as if she can go out to the local pub every now and again for some cheer. You gotta help her out!

❧ CatL♥ve 44 ❧

If your cat has persistent behavioral problems, it is probably a sign that he is unhappy for some reason. If you can't figure out the cause of the problem, take your cat to the vet or to a cat therapist (yes, they do exist). Kitty's happiness must be maintained at all costs!

❈ CatL♥ve 45 ❈

If you can afford it, you might think about trying out that pet psychic you saw on the community access channel. Wouldn't you like to know exactly what your cat's thinking? Well, maybe not...

❀ CatL♥ve 46 ❀

Have you tried the scoop variety
of litter? I think you'll like it.
Not only will your home smell
better, but waste disposal will be
easier and, overall, things will
just be a whole lot more
plea-*scent* for kitcat!

❧ CatL♥ve 47 ❧

Buy a sturdy and "cat-friendly" carrier for your cat. When you transport her to the vet and other destinations, it's no wonder she meows incessantly if you've packed her in a cardboard box without "windows"!

❧ CatL♥ve 48 ❧

When your new cat mother is nursing her kittens, she requires more than three times her normal intake of food, so feed her as much as she wants! (And then make arrangements to have her spayed!)

❤ CatLove 49 ❤

If, for whatever reason, you've decided not to have kids, why not adopt another cat! It's a lot less expensive—and relatively hassle-free—compared to supporting a child for 18 or more years!

❧ CatL♥ve 50 ❧

If your cat is very ill, and your vet suggests that he be put to sleep, please get a second opinion! If a friend of mine had listened to the first vet she consulted, her 13-year-old baby would have been put to sleep several years ago. Fortunately, she went to another vet, the cat had surgery, and he is now a happy, healthy 17-year-old!

❧ CatL♥ve 51 ❧

If your cat likes to sleep a lot, let her! You need your 8 hours, and your cat needs her...18 hours!

❧ CatL♥ve 52 ❧

To ward off furballs, you may have heard that giving your cat a little butter every day helps. Well, this is true. And, your cat will lick his chops with joy! (Petromalt works well, too!)

❧ CatL♥ve 53 ❧

If you've just adopted a new kitten, and you already have another cat, put the kitten behind closed doors in another room for at least a half hour while your older cat gets used to kitty's smell. The fur will probably still fly for a few weeks, but initiating the two slowly will help the situation a bit.

❧ CatL♥ve 54 ❧

If some sort of domestic change is in the works, such as a move or a vacation, make plans ahead of time for taking care of kitty. Rushing around in a panic trying to figure out what to do with the cat won't make you or her very happy!

❀ CatL♥ve 55 ❀

When you're watching your favorite show, and your cat is on top of the TV with his paw hanging over your favorite TV star's face, you might be tempted to move said cat's paw. But please don't. You'll make kitty mad.

❁ CatL♥ve 56 ❁

Does your cat have a problem with ear mites? To relieve his "ear"-ita-tion, in addition to using the drops that you need to get from your vet, also dab the inside of his ear with a cotton swab to remove any visible mites. This will speed up your cat's recovery.

❀ CatL♥ve 57 ❀

If you have a Christmas tree in your home during the holidays, make sure that your cat doesn't drink the water at the base of the tree. There are toxins that seep out of the tree into this water that can make her very sick.

❧ CatL♥ve 58 ☙

Now when it comes to drinking out of the toilet (your cat, not you), I vote no on this practice. All sorts of bacteria are breeding in this area, so protect your cat from himself, and keep the lid closed—especially if you have blue water in the tank!

❀ CatL♥ve 59 ❀

If you buy a new piece of furniture for your home, let your cat be the first to initiate it. After all, it wouldn't feel like a real part of your home if it didn't have a half-inch of cat hair on it, right?

❈ CatL♥ve 60 ❈

If you move your indoor/outdoor cat to a new home, keep her inside for at least a month so she can get used to the smell of her new residence. She uses scent to find her way back home when she is outside. (When cats rub their chins against objects in your home, they're "marking" their place, so to speak.)

❈ CatL♥ve 61 ❈

If you do let your cat outside at any time, make sure he's wearing a collar and I.D. tag with your name, address, and current telephone number on it. If he got lost, you'd be heartbroken!

❈ CatL♥ve 62 ❈

Think about taking your cat on vacation with you. There are actually motels and bed-and-breakfast inns throughout the country that *cat-er* to cats on the road. Ask your cat-friendly travel agent for details.

 CatL♥ve 63 ☙

You needn't bathe your indoor cat; she does a fine job of licking and grooming herself. The only exception is if she gets into something really dirty—like that family of dust bunnies under your bed!

❀ CatL♥ve 64 ❀

Always use positive reinforcement when you try to train your cat. Never, ever hit him for any reason. A loud "No!" or a handy water-filled plant-sprayer or water pistol is the only punishment that needs to be meted out. (Sometimes tapping his nose gently with two fingers also works.)

❧ CatL♥ve 65 ❧

When choosing a kitten from a litter, cat shelter, or pet store, look for the cat that seems bright-eyed, outgoing, and willing to be held. He will no doubt make the best companion for you!

❧ CatL♥ve 66 ❧

When there is a family emergency, please don't forget about
your kitty; she still needs to be
fed and cared for. After all,
when you're sick, doesn't she
always "take care" of you?
You know exactly what I mean,
don't you?

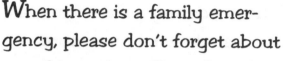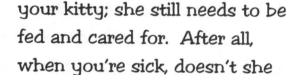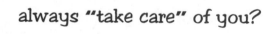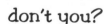

❀ CatL♥ve 67 ❀

Spread the word about the joys of cat ownership. There are a lot of orphaned cats out there, and a lot of people don't even realize how much they'd enjoy adopting one (or more) cats until they try it. Your cat (who knows all) will silently thank you for your efforts!

❀ CatL♥ve 68 ❀

Take lots of photos of your cat and display them prominently in your home. She's as much of a family member as anyone, so let everybody know it!

❀ CatL♥ve 69 ❀

Stay calm—don't get mad—when your cat is regurgitating a big 'ol furball on your new rug. It's normal for cats (especially long-haired ones) to expel furballs every few weeks, and kitty really has no control over where she does it. (*Hint*: If you let the furball dry for a few hours, it's a lot easier to pick up and probably won't even leave a stain.)

❖ CatL♥ve 70 ❖

Does your cat ever wake you up in the middle of the night by purring loudly and enthusiastically licking your nose? Well, if so, and you happen to know what this means, please let me know! (Maybe I'm supposed to do something for her in return?)

❀ CatL♥ve 71 ❀

Your cat just loves to be stroked and scratched lightly from his head down to his tail, so do it often. She kneads to be needed!

❀ CatL♥ve 72 ❀

The best way to give a cat a pill (so you both don't get totally stressed out) is to hold his head firmly with one hand while drawing it back so the mouth opens. Then, plant the pill on the back of the tongue and shut the mouth. Rub his throat gently to encourage him to swallow. Good luck!

❧ CatL♥ve 73 ❧

Don't use rug shampoos, disinfectants, pesticides, or other household products of this kind without checking the labels carefully. Some of these items are extremely toxic to pets.

❧ CatL♥ve 74 ❧

If your cat tends to scratch you a lot while you're playing with him, give a little yelp every time he does so. He'll get the message because he doesn't want to hurt you–he loves you!

❤ CatL♥ve 75 ❤

If you have more than one cat, be sure to give them the same amount of attention and love— it seems that whenever I talk lovingly to one of my cats and stroke her, my other little sweetie will run up and demand equal time. Cats, like children, get jealous, too!

❧ CatL♥ve 76 ❧

Play games with string and balls and the like that will allow your cat to run and jump. If your cat sleeps all the time, maybe it's because she doesn't have anybody to play with. Boo hoo.

❀ CatL♥ve 77 ❀

Does your cat like to drink out
of the bathroom sink faucet like
it's a water fountain? Do him a
favor, and let him do so whenever he requests it. Cats don't have
that much variety in their lives,
so every diversion helps!

 CatLove 78

Learn to recognize the signs that your cat is sick. The first sign is usually loss of appetite, followed by runny eyes and a dull, matted coat. If she's coughing, sneezing, or vomiting, a trip to the vet is a must!

 CatLove 79

When you massage your cat, use your nails gently instead of just using your fingers; he'll feeeeellll good!

☙ CatL♥ve 80 ☙

Have I mentioned giving your cat an extra dose of love today? It doesn't cost anything and SHE DESERVES IT!

☙ CatL♥ve 81 ☙

Train your cat to avoid kitchen countertops. Hot stoves and sharp utensils can hurt kitcat!

❖ CatL♥ve 82 ❖

Your cat loves to be stroked behind her ears, because this is one of those places she can't reach with her tongue. Your touch may remind her of her mother's caresses!

❖ CatL♥ve 83 ❖

If you live on a farm or a ranch and you let your cat roam outside, take him to the vet for regular checkups. He is much more apt to pick up fleas, ticks, and other things that become attached to him than an indoor cat would.

❧ CatL♥ve 84 ❧

Really listen to the quality of your cat's different meows. If you're a cat owner in the know, you'll soon figure out which meow means "I'm hungry," "Give me love," "Play with me," or the ever-popular "Go away and let me sleep."

❖ CatL♥ve 85 ❖

If you have to move to a new apartment for some reason and are having a hard time finding a residence that accepts cats, you might offer the landlord of the building you're interested in an extra security deposit. This could sway someone to ease the "No Pets" rule.

❀ CatL♥ve 86 ❀

This point bears repeating: Your cat runs your home; you just live there. When she "head-butts" you on the leg, she's "marking" you with pheromones—a scent that makes you her property... and don't you forget it!

❀ CatL♥ve 87 ❀

If you have a party at your home, do your cat a favor and put him in one of his favorite rooms with food, water, and his litter box...then close the door. You can't assume that everyone who comes in contact with your beloved will bestow the respect he deserves upon him. Who knows how some inebriated cat-hater might treat him! (Naturally, a person such as this would not be a friend of yours—merely an uninvited gate-crasher!)

❖ CatL♥ve 88 ❖

If your cat has suddenly stopped using the litter box properly, there is probably a medical problem that is causing him to misbehave. Talk to your vet as soon as possible.

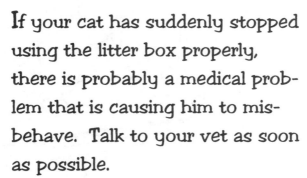

❀ CatL♥ve 89 ❀

If your cat seems to ignore TV, you might buy one of those videos featuring birds chirping and flying about. My cat sat in a chair for 15 minutes, transfixed by all the birdies on the screen. It was almost too cute!

❧ CatL♥ve 90 ❧

If you or one of your housemates is allergic to cats, but a catlover nonetheless, consider adopting a Sphinx cat (a Canadian
hairless). They're very sweet and loving (if
not great beauties). Hey...it's what's inside
that counts!

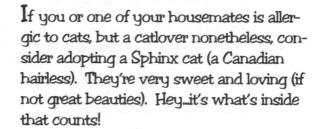

❧ CatL♥ve 91 ❧

Put some extra milk in your morning
cereal so when you get to the bottom
of the bowl, kitty can take up the
slack. Slurp, slurp!

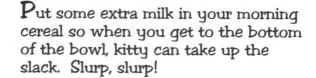

❀ CatL❤ve 92 ❀

After you do your laundry, leave out the basket so your kitcat can sleep on the warm, clean clothes. So what's a little cat hair among friends!? (You'll probably want to always have a lint brush on hand.)

❀ CatL♥ve 93 ❀

Vacuum the fur off your *fur*-niture so your cat has a nice, clean spot to mess up again. She pre-*furs* it that way!

❀ CatL♥ve 94 ❀

Honor your cat with a feline altar. You know you've got all those cat figurines, photos, stuffed animals, and more lying around your home. So, put them out for all the world to see!

❧ CatL♥ve 95 ❧

If you must board your cat, really shop around until you find a place that's warm, spotless, and where he will get the attention he deserves.

❧ CatL♥ve 96 ❧

If your cat is being particularly finicky and won't eat her regular food, don't force it on her. Cats have moods, too. Why not give her a special treat today!

❀ CatL♥ve 97 ❀

If your cat has been declawed, never let him outside by himself. He won't be able to defend himself against unfriendly critters!

❀ CatL♥ve 98 ❀

Give your cat tartar-control treats on a regular basis if she'll eat them. Cats can get plaque, too, you know!

❀ CatL♥ve 99 ❀

If you are entertaining cat-loving overnight guests who miss their feline, encourage your cat to sleep with them to keep them company. They will all feel warm and fuzzy and, hey, it's the neighborly thing to do!

❧ CatL♥ve 100 ❧

Does your cat love lying between the pages of a good book, as mine does? Why not set aside a few books that are exclusively his to "get into"!

❧ CatL♥ve 101 ❧

On very hot summer days, rub some ice on your cat's body. It can be very uncomfortable wearing a fur coat when it's 90 degrees outside!

❧ CatL♥ve 102 ❧

Never leave your cat unattended in your car! The temperature in your vehicle on a sunny day can get up to 10 to 20 degrees higher than the temperature outside, resulting in severe dehydration—and even death—to your cat!

❥ CatL♥ve 103 ❥

Forget that insulting Ogden Nash poem, and remember this paraphrased version: *The best thing about a kitten is that...It eventually grows into a cat!* Your cat will appreciate the sentiment!

❥ CatL♥ve 104 ❥

Before you cook a whole chicken, pull out the kidney, chop it up into little pieces, and give it to your cat. He will be in feline heaven!

❧ CatL♥ve 105 ❧

To calm your cat when she is nervous, sit her on your lap, cup her face with your hand, and gently rub your finger down the side of her nose.

❧ CatL♥ve 106 ❧

Don't ever let anyone tell you that cats have no emotions. When you've been away for a long time, doesn't your cat act somewhat angry? Be particularly sensitive to his feelings— maybe a treat and some extra lovin' will help bring him around.

 CatL♥ve 107

When your clothes are drying, clear off the top of the dryer so your cat can lie on the warm surface. (She likes the vibration from the dryer, too!)

 CatL♥ve 108

If you live in a snowy climate and you let your cat outdoors in the winter, be ready with a warm cloth to wrap kitty in (and, if possible, a cozy fire in the fireplace) when he comes back in.

❧ CatL♥ve 109 ❧

When you do wonderful things for other people and cats, you are paying respect to your own cat, too, so...if you know any elderly or disabled (or just lonely) persons who could use some loving companionship, find out if they would like to adopt a cat. If so, you might want to help them do so and advise them on buying litter, a litter box, a food/water dish, and an initial supply of food to start them out. Cats can change people's lives!

❧ CatL♥ve 110 ❧

When you open a can of tuna, instead of draining the water or oil into the sink, pour it over your cat's dry or wet food. What a special treat for your kitcat!

❧ CatL♥ve 111 ❧

At any time of the year, but especially in the winter, keep the blinds or shades open so the sun can come in. Your cat loves to bask in the warmth of the sunshine! Also, he loves to watch the birds and make bird noises right back at 'em!

❧ CatL♥ve 112 ❧

If you live in a house and have
an indoor/outdoor cat, you
might want to install a cat flap
to allow her some independence.
But, be careful of neighborhood
cats and other critters following
kitty into "her" home!

❀ CatL♥ve 113 ❀

When you're out of town, call home and talk to your answering machine for a while so your cat can hear the sound of her Mom or Dad's voice. It will make her feel less lonely.

❀ CatL♥ve 114 ❀

If you use window fans in your home, be sure that they have some type of protective shield so that your cat's paws and tail do not get caught in the blades of the fan. That would be very uncool!

❧ CatL♥ve 115 ❧

*C*heck your closets and drawers before closing them. Your cat has a sneaky way of disappearing into these areas when you're not looking, and you wouldn't want to leave home for an extended period with him trapped in a tight spot without food, water, or a litter box!

 CatL♥ve 116

If your cat squirms a lot when he is being brushed or combed, talk softly or sing to him while he's being groomed. You might also want to give him a little treat after he's gone through this "hair-raising" ordeal!

❧ CatL♥ve 117 ❧

If you own a Dustbuster, try running it over your cat's body gently. Even though she may be frightened by the upright cleaner, most cats love to be cleaned with this smaller version of a vacuum cleaner. It's a good way to remove excess hair, and judging by the way my cat reacts, it must feel pretty good, too!

❖ CatL♥ve 118 ❖

Clip your cat's toenails frequently so she doesn't catch them on rugs or upholstered or wicker furniture. When a cat tears a nail, it really hurts—just like when you tear one (Me-OW)!

❖ CatL♥ve 119 ❖

If your veterinarian doesn't automatically mail you a notice regarding annual examinations, use your cat's birthday as the date when you take him in for shots. A healthy indoor cat can live up to 20 years these days!

❧ CatL♥ve 120 ❧

Cats generally detest leaving the comfort and familiarilty of their homes. So, when you or your friends are away, take care of their pets in their absence, and your friends will no doubt reciprocate.

❧ CatL♥ve 121 ❧

If your cat enjoys sitting in screened windows, be sure the screens are locked securely in place. I'll never forget the day my parents' cat fell two stories when the screen in their living room blew out on a stormy day.
The woman in the apartment below saw a cat flying past her window! (Fortunately, Snowshoes the cat still had 8 lives left!)

❧ CatL♥ve 122 ❧

Many cats are utterly fascinated by small children and enjoy playing with them (as long as the kids don't pull their tails, etc.). Maybe it's because toddlers are more "down to earth" and the cats like to be on the same level with their playmates. Whatever the reason, encourage this type of kinship—it could turn into a lifelong love affair.

❁ CatL♥ve 123 ❁

A happy cat owner usually translates to a happy cat. So, meditate, do affirmations regularly, think positive thoughts, and do good things for your fellow citizens...and happiness will be yours...and your cat's!

❖ CatL♥ve 124 ❖

Keep a cat care book in your home library for emergencies. There are many great books out there that give very useful cat-related medical advice (both preventive and otherwise), and if something happens to your cat and you can't reach your vet immediately, one of these books can be a lifesaver.

❁ CatL♥ve 125 ❁

If you decide to declaw your indoor cat's front paws (I'm not going to get into the controversy of whether this is inhumane or not—that's for you to decide), make sure you use shredded newspaper instead of conventional litter for a few weeks after he comes home from the vet so his little paws won't get infected with litter particles.

❖ CatL♥ve 126 ❖

A wonderful thing you can do for all cats is to donate time or money to some of the nonprofit organizations, centers, and shelters in your community that rescue and care for cats. Just one visit to one of these places will melt your heart and inspire you to help out in some way.

❀ CatL♥ve 127 ❀

When your cat is sitting on your lap or when you're talking to her as she's resting on another surface, make eye contact with her as you speak. Cats appreciate this as much as humans do, and she will reward you by giving you purrs and contented blinks of the eye!

❤ CatL♥ve 128 ❤

In the same way that you "childproof" a home, do the same for your cat. He can get into lethal disinfectants and poisons in bottom cabinets just like kids can!

❤ CatL♥ve 129 ❤

Another way to cat-proof your home is to mount electrical cords on your wall with a velcro-type fastening device so your cat will not be tempted to bite into cords that are lying on the ground. Such behavior can lead to serious burns to the mouth and face.

❧ CatL♥ve 130 ❧

Even if you use the scoop form of litter, your litter box needs to be completely cleaned out at least once a month. Scrub it with soap and water, and dry it thoroughly before refilling it. Your cat will appreciate it even if he doesn't put it into words!

❧ CatL♥ve 131 ❧

If you have more than one cat, let them run around your home and play with each other without interference. My cats chase each other back and forth across my apartment every night around 10:30 and then wrestle for a few minutes. I just let them be. Cats need to get out their aggressions just like humans, after all!

❧ CatL♥ve 132 ❧

Do you ever have your home or apartment cleaned or have repairs done while you're at work? If so, make sure you remind all service people not to let your indoor cat out. Also, make sure that the people you let into your home like cats. You wouldn't want some sadistic person to play "Kick the Cat" with your baby!

❀ CatL♥ve 133 ❀

When you get a new kitten or cat, give him a name that is cute, but not demeaning. Would you want to be called "Binky," "Seymour J. Catz," "Namby," "Tush Push," or some of the other embarrassing names I've heard? I don't think so.

❧ CatL♥ve 134 ❧

Leave your cat's whiskers exactly as they are. I once saw a guy start to cut his cat's whiskers because, as this unknowing cat-owner explained: "They're getting so long!" I educated him to the fact that whiskers reflect a cat's girth and are their "feelers" in the dark. Hallelujah! Kitty's whiskers were saved!

 CatL♥ve 135

If you are going to be away from home for a considerable length of time and will probably be home after dark, think about leaving a light on for your cat. It will soothe her while she's patiently (or impatiently) waiting for you to return.

 CatL♥ve 136

Stroke your cat under his chin frequently. The pleasure he derives from it is considerable. His look of gratitude will be worth every stroke!

❧ CatL♥ve 137 ❧

If you live in an area where earth-quakes, tornadoes, hurricanes, or other natural disasters occur, you might want to designate one person in your family as the cat care-taker—the one who will be specifi-cally responsible for seeing that your cat is taken care of in the event of one of these occurrences.

❖ CatL♥ve 138 ❖

You know how your cat loves to rub her chin against the things in your home? Well, make sure there aren't any sharp edges on coffee tables or other objects that could hurt kitty.

❖ CatL♥ve 139 ❖

Why don't you buy your cat one of those cat toys that looks like a fishing pole. I guarantee you it will become one of his favorites!

❧ CatL♥ve 140 ❧

If you have more than one cat, and they tend to lick each other's fur, this is an additional reason to comb or brush your cats daily. If you don't, they'll accumulate double the amount of furballs!

❧ CatL♥ve 141 ❧

If you have a swimming pool, discourage your cat from drinking out of it. Chlorine is not good for her delicate digestive system!

❀ CatL♥ve 142 ❀

Some cat owners only take their cats to the vet once a year to get vaccinations, but many vets only give shots at these times and don't do an annual exam as well. Make sure your cat is thoroughly examined each year *in addition* to getting the required immunization!

❀ CatL♥ve 143 ❀

Avoid picking your cat up by the scruff of the neck. This is something that cat mothers do with newborn kittens at times, but it is not appropriate or safe for humans to do to their cats. Think about how it would feel if someone picked _you_ up like that!

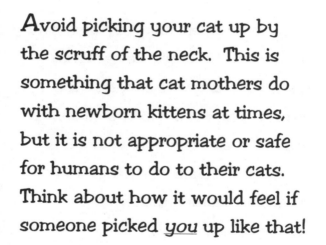

❤ CatL♥ve 144 ❤

If you don't know exactly when your cat's birthday is, make the day that you adopted her the day of celebration each year – and then pamper, pamper, pamper (even more than you usually do)!

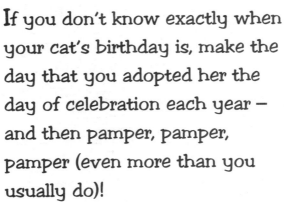

❧ CatL♥ve 145 ❧

If you think you're really going to enjoy that sliced turkey sandwich with your cat gazing up at you with those big eyes, think again. Take out a few pieces for him so you can both enjoy lunch!

❀ CatL♥ve 146 ❀

If your cat is severely overweight, please see a (good) vet. When I was a kid, I had a cat whose stomach touched the floor. Our vet (who obviously didn't know much), said, "Just feed her less." We finally took Samantha to a vet who specialized in cats, and it turned out she had a thyroid condition. After being given medication, she was trim and healthy in no time.

❧ CatL♥ve 147 ❧

If you keep your cat's litter box in your bathroom, be sure to leave the door open when you're taking a bath or shower (depending on your living situation). When your cat has to go, he's gotta go NOW!

 CatL♥ve 148

Make sure you don't leave a glass filled with water or milk lying out on a table. My cat once put her whole head in a mug to try to get to some water that was at the bottom, and then she got stuck, and couldn't get her head out! This could have been very dangerous if I hadn't been there to help her!

❧ CatL♥ve 149 ❧

When you get home from the supermarket, leave the empty brown paper grocery bags on the floor for a while, so your cat can play. But don't forget to let the cat out of the bag before you dispose of it!

❧ CatL♥ve 150 ❧

At Christmastime, if you tend to keep those beautiful red poinsettia plants around your home, be sure you keep them in a place that is inaccessible to your cat. These plants are toxic if eaten!

❧ CatL♥ve 151 ❧

When you take your cat on trips, put the cat carrier on the seat next to you (where your cat can see you) instead of on the back seat or the floor. The trip will be less traumatic for both of you!

❧ CatL♥ve 152 ❧

If you want your cat to use his scratching post (rather than your new sofa), try sprinkling some fresh catnip on it – he could become very attached to his post!

❧ CatL♥ve 153 ❧

Do you have a new kitten who loves to sleep in your hair at night? Well, that's okay – let her have her way. She'll grow out of it, and it doesn't bother you that much, does it? After all, that's her way of feeling warm, safe, and secure.

❧ CatL♥ve 154 ❧

If you have a dog that tends to eat up all of your cat's food before he can get to it, think about feeding your cat on a table or countertop that is too high for the dog to jump up on – kitty needs his food!

❀ CatL♥ve 155 ❀

Read the labels on the cat foods you buy. Those which are filled with all kinds of by-products and fillers may not be nutritionally sound. Check with your veterinarian or a knowledgeable pet store employee if you have questions about what's best for your kitcat.

❧ CatL♥ve 156 ❧

I like my cats to feel that they can walk anywhere they want in my home, but sometimes they tend to step on the answering machine, either turning it off or deleting messages. If this happens to you, try doing what I did: I put the answering machine in a cassette box (with a side opening). Now the cats can walk on top of the box without erasing the messages of my catl♥ving friends!

❖ CatL♥ve 157 ❖

Some humans love the smell of
gasoline, raspberries, or fried onions.
Your cat, however, would probably
be in seventh heaven if...you left your
sneakers or shoes lying around. She
loves to sniff them and put her paws
and head inside them—especially after
you've just taken them off!

❖ CatL♥ve 158 ❖

If you have a new kitten who is eating voraciously and is unusually fat, your kitten probably has worms – but don't despair – this is a problem that is easily curable with a shot or pills from your vet.

❖ CatL♥ve 159 ❖

On cold winter nights, lift up that comforter and let your cat sleep with you under the covers. It feels wonderful to have a warm, fuzzy body next to you, and your cat will love being that close to her beloved master or mistress.

❧ CatL♥ve 160 ❧

Do you have more than two cats,? Well, make sure you use two litter boxes instead of one. Even with the scoop-style litter, one litter box just won't cut it!

❧ CatL♥ve 161 ❧

If your cat has grime on him that only soap and water can remove, put him in the bathtub. Let him sit there and relax for a few minutes before you start "torturing" him with soap and lukewarm water. If you have sliding glass doors, he will be effectively trapped, so...good luck...and wear long sleeves to resist scratches!

❧ CatL♥ve 162 ❧

Designate a blanket for your cat's use and sprinkle some catnip on it so he becomes attached to it. Then, if for some reason you would prefer that he sleep in another room, you can lay down "his" blanket, and he might be more amenable to the change in scenery.

❀ CatL♥ve 163 ❀

They say cats don't take to water, but my little cat Dolly sure loves it! If your cat is the same way, let her enjoy playing with a thin stream of water that you let trickle out of the sink or bathtub. But don't forget to turn off the water after a minute or so — wasting water is a no-no!

❀ CatL♥ve 164 ❀

A good way to warm up your cat's canned food in a hurry after it's been in the refrigerator overnight is to microwave it for about 10 seconds. Kitty doesn't like to wait the 30 min-utes or so that it would normally take for her food to get to room temperature!

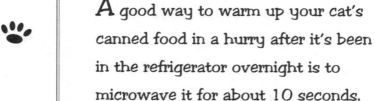

❧ CatL♥ve 165 ❧

Does your indoor cat tend to jump on the balcony of your home or apartment, making you very, very nervous? You might want to consider screening in the balcony so your cat can _see_ out, but not _get_ out!

❧ CatL♥ve 166 ❧

If you want to keep your home a little cleaner and also make your cat's paws more comfortable, think about getting a litter catcher. You can place it in front of your cat's litter box, and it will remove the litter from his paws after he's covered up his "work."

❦ CatL♥ve 167 ❦

Don't take your cat places that will scare her just because it seems like a cute thing to do. I once took my cat to the beach, thinking she'd enjoy a change of scenery, but she was so terrified by the waves and the sand that she shrieked at the top of her little lungs. It was a CAT-astrophe!

❧ CatL♥ve 168 ❧

If you are planning on traveling with your cat by air, be sure your cat is wearing an up-to-date I.D. tag, and try not to travel during very hot or cold weather, as the baggage compartment where your cat may be kept may not be heated or air-conditioned.

❧ CatL♥ve 169 ❧

If you decide to hire a pet-sitter, make sure you get references, and then be certain that he or she agrees to clean the litter box, refill the food and water bowls, administer any necessary medications, and give your cat some love and attention for at least a half-hour per visit. (And don't forget to leave your vet's name and number, as well as a number where you can be reached in case of emergency.)

❦ CatL♥ve 170 ❦

The next time you bring home new shoes, remember to leave out the empty shoe boxes for a while so your kitty can jump in. If your cat is like mine, she'll wedge herself into the smallest box no matter how "substantial" (i.e., fat) she is!

❖ CatL♥ve 171 ❖

Check out your cat's teeth on a regular basis. Cats can get tartar buildup and plaque just like humans, but your cat (unless he has extra-special powers) won't be able to tell you if he has a toothache, so it's up to you to check him out every once in a while.

❧ CatL♥ve 172 ❧

If your cat tends to look forlorn and even cry when you leave for work in the morning, you might consider putting down her food for the day right before you leave or getting her involved with one of her favorite toys so she doesn't notice you're leaving. Now, if *you're* the one who looks forlorn and cries when you have to leave your cat, that's another problem altogether (although *purr*-fectly understandable)!

❧ CatL♥ve 173 ❧

Before you let your vaccinated cat play with neighbor cats, talk to their owners to make sure they have had their feline distemper and leukemia shots, too. Vaccinations are not 100 percent effective, so even a cat who has had his shots can be infected by a sick friend.

❧ CatL♥ve 174 ❧

For the sake of your cat and all pets, you might think about buying a reference guide (through a cat magazine or your pet store) that reveals which manufacturers do and do not test their products on animals. Think about how you'd feel if your cat was being used in an experiment to test mascara!

❧ CatL♥ve 175 ❧

If a glass object happens to break in your home, be sure to sweep up the glass and then vacuum, so particles don't get into your cat's paws. Another effective way to pick up small glass particles is to use wet paper towels. The glass adheres to the towels, and then you can dispose of the towels easily. At this point, you can use a Dustbuster to pick up any particles you may have missed.

❧ CatL♥ve 176 ❧

Don't you just love it when your cat greets you at the door when you come home after a hard day's work? To make this a regular habit, give him a little treat when you walk in or just smother him with lots and lots of love. Chances are you'll see his sweet little whiskered face beaming up at you every day when you walk in!

❧ CatL♥ve 177 ❧

Subscribe to at least one cat
magazine so you can keep up on
the latest advances in cat-related
news, medical information, and
other feline tidbits. Your cat will
benefit if you're an owner in
the know!

❧ CatL♥ve 178 ❧

Do you really want to make your cat happy? Of course you do, or you wouldn't be reading this book! Well, have I got a tip for you: Pull out an emery board and start filing your nails. This seemingly simple act turns both my cats into ecstatic, purring sweet-hearts, crawling all over me and rolling over with joy. I don't know why...but it happens every time! (Believe it or not, one of my cats also reacts this way when I floss my teeth!)

❧ CatL♥ve 179 ❧

If, for some reason, you need to get your cat out of your home in a hurry, put him in a pillowcase for easy, fast transporting. He won't be too happy about it, but it will get the job done!

❧ CatL♥ve 180 ❧

Find a place to board your cat (or bring her to work if you can) when you get your home fumigated. Never, under any circumstances, leave her at home when spraying is being done!

❧ CatL♥ve 181 ❧

If your indoor cat accidentally gets out and you can't find him, alert your neighbors to look for him, notify your local cat shelter, put an ad in the "Lost and Found" section of your newspaper, post notices with his name and photo, and walk around your neighborhood yelling his name! Losing your baby would just be CAT-astrophic!

❧ CatL♥ve 182 ❧

Avoid giving your cat the tuna that you buy for yourself. He may become addicted to the strong taste and smell and refuse to eat anything else. Not only that, but tuna is not nutritionally complete and wouldn't be healthful to give your baby on a regular basis.

 CatL♥ve 183

Does your cat pester you with meows and whimpers while you're eating? If so, you might put her in a separate room during these times. She'll eventually learn that if she wants to hang out with the family, she'll have to behave herself at mealtime.

 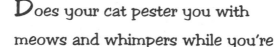 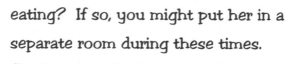 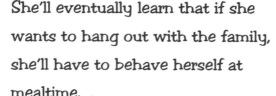

❀ CatL♥ve 184 ❀

If you find that your cat is over-grooming himself, this could be a result of some sort of stressful situation. Try to determine what is troubling your puss, as overgrooming can lead to skin conditions such as eczema and dermatitis. Your vet may have to prescribe tranquilizers if your TLC fails!

❧ CatL♥ve 185 ❧

If you have two or more cats, and one of them passes away, the other cat(s) might go through a grieving period that is similar to your own. Be extra attentive to your feline(s), and think about adopting a new cat in the near future to keep your cat(s) company.

❧ CatL♥ve 186 ❧

If you intend to breed your cat, ask personnel at local cat shows or breeding clubs to supply you with names of reliable and knowledgable breeders in your area.

❀ CatL♥ve 187 ❀

Has your cat been sleeping with you for most of her life? And, for one reason or another, is her space on your bed now being taken up by a human? If this is the case, your cat may be rather miffed by this turn of events, to say the least. Think about making her a special bed of her own that is right beside your bed. It's the next best thing to bedding there!

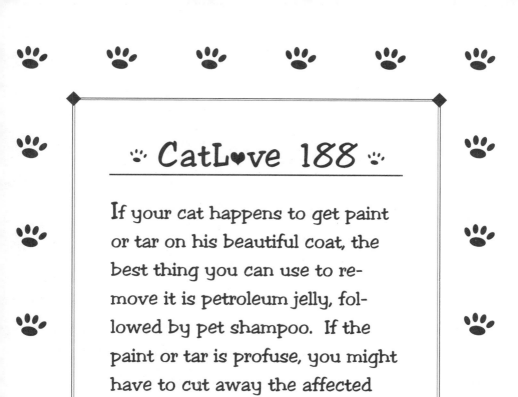

❖ CatL♥ve 188 ❖

If your cat happens to get paint or tar on his beautiful coat, the best thing you can use to remove it is petroleum jelly, followed by pet shampoo. If the paint or tar is profuse, you might have to cut away the affected area with a scissors.

❧ CatL♥ve 189 ❧

If your little sweetie is sick, you might
want to prepare a special "sick bed"
for him. Put him in a blanket-filled
box in a quiet corner of his favorite
room, and you might even think about
putting a hot water bottle filled with
lukewarm water in his get-well spot.
He will appreciate your loving care!

 CatL♥ve 190

Do you and your cat live in a very sunny, hot climate? If so, and if you allow your cat to roam outside, some sunblock applied to her ears will prevent sunburn on this sensitive area. (Your cat will be especially prone to burning if she is light in color.)

❖ CatL♥ve 191 ❖

Do you meditate on a regular basis? I do, and I find that my cats tend to jump on my lap and purr while I'm in this relaxed state. Maybe this is a sign that cats enjoy the peaceful vibe that emanates from a happy, tranquil person — try it sometime!

CatL♥ve 192 ⛅

On extremely hot days, put your cat in the bathtub (sans water)—she'll love the feel of the cold porcelain on her fur!

⛅ CatL♥ve 193 ⛅

To add some extra nutrition to your cat's diet, you might cook some fresh meat mixed with vegetables such as peas, carrots, or green beans; or mix some cooked egg with the meat.

❖ CatL♥ve 194 ❖

When you are planning to move to a new home or apartment, keep your cat's needs in mind. Does the apartment have a lot of windows for kitty to sit in, and a balcony that will allow her to get some fresh air? Does the home have an enclosed yard that will allow her to play outside but not stray away from home? Think about it.

☙ CatL♥ve 195 ☙

If you are fortunate enough to have a very docile cat who likes to be carried in your arms on walks or other forays outside the home, be sure to keep a harness and leash on him at all times. Any loud noise could cause your cat to jump out of your arms in a split second, and he might dart out into the street before you know it.

 CatL♥ve 196

Is your cat pregnant? Since you are a responsible cat owner, I'm sure you plan on spaying her just as soon as you can after she gives birth, but in the meantime, you can make her pregnancy a healthy one by feeding her a well-balanced diet and gradually increasing her food intake during the last four weeks of gestation.

CatLove 197

Is there a neighbor animal who is continually "bullying" your beloved feline? First, talk to the offending animal's owner to see if you can work out a solution, but if this doesn't work, you might have to talk to an animal control officer or...think about keeping your cat indoors.

CatLove 198

If you happen to have a heat lamp in your bathroom or other room in your home, let your cat sleep under it. He'll love soaking up the warmth!

❧ CatL♥ve 199 ❧

Does your cat torture your toilet paper roll, spearing it and clawing at it so it looks like Swiss cheese? Why not just give her her own roll to play with on the ground—it will make both of you a lot happier!

❖ CatL♥ve 200 ❖

Try not to have things around your home that will annoy your cat. If he jumps every time your door buzzer sounds or your phone rings, you might think about making some modifications to preclude such disruptions. (No, I'm not *kitting!*)

CatL♥ve 201

If you happen to notice that your cat's white "third eyelid" is showing, this could be a sign that she is suffering from worms, diarrhea, or some other ailment. Take her to the vet as soon as possible.

 CatL♥ve 202

I've mentioned getting your cat a kitty companion, but you might also think about getting her a canine companion. A puppy probably won't intimidate your cat, and will probably become her best buddy as they grow up together.

❧ CatL♥ve 203 ❧

Keep the area where your cat eats as clean as possible (especially during the summer months), checking for ants or other critters that might crawl into your cat's food and water bowls. On very hot days, you might drop an ice cube into the water bowl to cool kitty off when she seeks to quench her thirst.

❖ CatL♥ve 204 ❖

 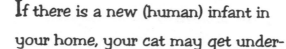

If there is a new (human) infant in your home, your cat may get understandably jealous of all the attention that the baby is getting. Make a point of giving your cat some extra TLC, and say his name a lot while you're doing it. He'll learn that there's enough love to go around for everyone!

 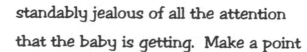
 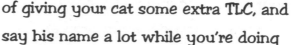
 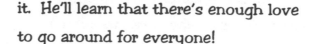

⋆ CatL♥ve 205 ⋆

After you brush your cat, if you gently rub her down with a piece of velvet or silk or a chamois cloth, her coat will be healthy, shiny, and oh-so-pettable.

⋆ CatL♥ve 206 ⋆

Respect your cat's inalienable right to have his own space, indulge in his own moods, and engage in activities that make him happy. For example, if on one partic- ular day, he chooses to curl up in the cor- ner of a dark room for hours at a time, leave him be. He can be playful, frisky, and attentive to you on another day!

❧ CatL♥ve 207 ❧

Does your cat like to sit right next to your computer while you work at home? If so, why not make it easy for her to do so. Clear a space on your desk so your baby doesn't have to lie on notebooks, pencil points, staplers, and other uncomfortable office supplies.

❖ CatL♥ve 208 ❖

Pick up this book periodically (and, of course, give it to your cat-loving friends as gifts) so you will remember to do wonderful things for your cat on a regular basis. It's easy to take the love, warmth, companionship, and loyalty that your cat gives you for granted. Doing special things for him will remind you that your cat is an extremely important and unique part of your life!

❖ CatL♥ve 209 ❖

Make your own list of wonderful things to do for your cat that specifically apply to your own little angel. Both you and your cat will reap the benefits!

❊ CatL♥ve 210 ❊

And, finally, scratch her fuzzy neck, kiss the top of her little head, rub her arching back...Hug his warm, furry body; cuddle with him, shower him with love...do everything you can to make your cat(s) happy...*they will always be your beloved babies!*

ARE'NT CATS THE <u>GREATEST</u>?!!!

If you and your cat would like to be eligible for inclusion in my next cat book, and perhaps be the lucky entrant whose cat(s) is/are chosen to appear on the book's cover, please submit this form, your written entry, and an engaging color photo of your cat(s)— no smaller than 3"x5", no larger than 8"x10"— to: Jill Kramer Cat Book, Hay House, Inc., P.O. Box 6204, Carson, CA 90749-6204.

All entries must be submitted to Hay House by December 1, 1995 and will become the sole property of the publisher. Entries/photos will not be returned; however, you will receive written notification if your entry and photo have been selected for inclusion in the book. The decision regarding the selection of the "cover cat" will be made at the sole discretion of the editor.

On a separate piece of paper (please type or print legibly), tell me about a WONDERFUL THING YOU'VE DONE FOR YOUR CAT(S) in 75 words or less. Please attach your entry and cat(s)' photo with this form by 12/1/95. (Photocopied forms are acceptable.)

Your name
_____

Your cat(s)' name, age, and sex
_____

_____

Address
_____

Day phone _____ Eve phone _____

I hereby give my permission for my name, city and state name, and my cats' name(s) to be used for inclusion in this book. I release all rights to the enclosed photo and any other information that I have submitted, which shall remain the sole property of Hay House, Inc. I understand that if my written entry and cat photo are used in this book, I WILL NOT BE ENTITLED TO ANY MONIES OR REMUNERATION OF ANY KIND, either prior to or subsequent to publication and sale.

_____

Signature _____ Date _____

ABOUT THE AUTHOR

When Jill Kramer was 8 years old, a strange cat wandered into her backyard in Ambler, Pennsylvania. After it was determined that the cat's apathetic owners didn't want to keep "Puss," Jill's family adopted her, thus beginning the author's lifelong love affair with these furry angels. Puss begat Junior (a calico cutie who remained with the Kramer family), and Friskie and Cutie, who moved in with the family next door. (And then Puss was spayed!)

After the untimely car-related deaths of Puss and Junior on the mean streets of Ambler (a good case for keeping your cat indoors), Jill's family adopted Samantha and Selma Ann—two of the sweetest cats east of the Mississippi, who lived long and happy lives. After moving to Southern California, Jill adopted Sage and Dolly, currently the feline loves of her life.

And that's all you really need to know about the author.

We hope you enjoyed this Hay House book. If you would like
to receive a free catalog featuring additional Hay House books
and products, or if you would like information about the
Hay Foundation, please write to:

Hay House, Inc.
1154 E. Dominguez St.
P.O. Box 6204
Carson, CA 90749-6204

or call:
(800) 654-5126